MW00906333

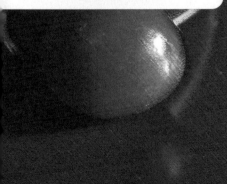

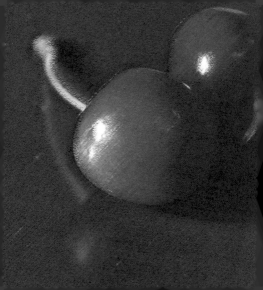

With Love to:

From:

The Gift of LOVE

©Scandinavia Publishing House
Drejervej 15,3 DK-Copenhagen NV
Denmark
Tel. +45-3531 0330
www.scanpublishing.dk
info@scanpublishing.dk

Edited and designed by Ben Alex

ISBN 978-87-7247-062-7

THE GIFT OF
LOVE

QUOTES FROM AROUND THE WORLD

scandinavia

Love is the
beauty of the soul.

ST. AUGUSTINE

He who wants
to do good
knocks at the gate;
he who loves
finds the door open.

Rabindranath Tagore

To love is like to live –
all reason is against it,
and all healthy instinct for it.

SAMUEL BUTLER

I have found that
when I silently commune
with people they give up
their secrets – if you
love them enough.

GEORGE WASHINGTON CARVER

We are shaped
and fashioned by
what we love.

GOETHE

Only in love
are unity and duality
not in conflict.

RABINDRANATH TAGORE

It is astonishing
how little one feels alone
when one loves.

JOHN BULWER

No cord or cable
can draw so forcibly,
or bind so fast,
as love can do
with a single thread.

ROBERT BURTON

Love dies only
when growth stops.

PEARL S. BUCK

With love
one can live
even without
happiness.

FEODOR DOSTOEVSKY

Love,
with very young people,
is a heartless business.
We drink at that age from
thirst, or to get drunk;
it is only later in life that we
occupy ourselves with the
individuality of our wine.

ISAK DINESEN

For a crowd
is not company;
and faces are but
a gallery of pictures;
and talk but a
tinkling cymbal,
where there is no love.

SIR FRANCIS BACON

I don't want to live.
I want to love first,
and live incidentally.

ZELDA FITZGERALD

Everything is,
everything exists,
only because I love.
Everything is united by it alone.
Love is God, and to die means
that I, a particle of love,
shall return to the general
and eternal source.

LEO TOLSTOY

Love is the final end
of the world's history,
the Amen of the universe.

Novalis Hardenberg

Love knows
hidden paths.

GERMAN PROVERB

Even as love crowns you
so shall he crucify you.
Even as he is for your growth
so is he for your pruning.

KHALIL GIBRAN

A life without love,
without the presence
of the beloved,
is nothing but a
mere magic-lantern show.
We draw out slide after slide,
swiftly tiring of each,
and pushing it back
to make haste for the next.

GOETHE

Love is a portion
of the soul itself,
and it is of the same nature
as the celestial breathing
of the atmosphere
of paradise.

VICTOR HUGO

For one human being
to love another:
that is perhaps the most
difficult of our tasks;
the ultimate, the last test and proof,
the work for which all other work
is but preparation.

RAINER MARIA RILKE

The reduction of the universe
to a single being,
the expansion of a single being
even to God, this is love.

VICTOR HUGO

How on earth are you
ever going to explain in
terms of chemistry and
physics so important a
biological phenomenon
as first love?

ALBERT EINSTEIN

There is always
some madness in love.
But there is also always
some reason in madness.

FRIEDRICH NIETZSCHE

Gravitation can not
be held responsible for
people falling in love.

ALBERT EINSTEIN

Put your hand
on a hot stove for a minute, and it
seems like an hour.
Sit with a pretty girl for an hour,
and it seems like a minute.
THAT'S relativity.

ALBERT EINSTEIN

Love is always
bestowed as a gift –
freely, willingly, and
without expectation.
We don't love to be loved;
we love to love.

LEO BUSCAGLIA

We are all born for love.
It is the principle of existence,
and its only end.

BENJAMIN DISRAELI

Darkness cannot
drive out darkness;
only light can do that.
Hate cannot drive out hate;
only love can do that.

Martin Luther King Jr

Love consists in this,
that two solitudes protect
and touch and greet
each other.

RAINER MARIA RILKE

Love is a fruit
in season at all times,
and within reach of
every hand.

MOTHER THERESA

Love's sweetest meanings
are unspoken; the full heart
knows no rhetoric of words.

CHRISTIAN NESTELL BOVEE

There is no surprise
more magical than the
surprise of being loved.
It is God's finger on
man's shoulder.

CHARLES MORGAN

Love is the only
sane and satisfactory
answer to the problem of
human existence.

ERIC FROMM

Love is a sweet tyranny,
because the lover endureth
his torments willingly.

PROVERB

Love has no desire
but to fulfill itself.
To melt and be like
a running brook that
sings its melody to the night.
To wake at dawn with a winged
heart and give thanks for
another day of loving.

KAHLIL GIBRAN

Who would give
a law to lovers?
Love is unto itself
a higher law.

BOETHIUS

Who,
being loved,
is poor?

OSCAR WILDE

The hours I spend with you
I look upon as sort of a
perfumed garden, a dim twilight,
and a fountain singing to it.
You and you alone make me feel
that I am alive. Other men it is
said have seen angels, but I have
seen thee and thou art enough.

GEORGE MOORE

Absence diminishes
small loves and
increases great ones,
as the wind blows out
the candle and fans
the bonfire.

LA ROCHEFOUCAULD

Many waters
cannot quench love,
neither can the floods
drown it.

SONG OF SOLOMON 8:7 (KJV)

Earth's the right place for love;
I don't know where
it's likely to go better.

ROBERT FROST

Love is
the wisdom of the fool
and the folly of the wise.

DR SAMUEL JOHNSON

Love is heaven,
and heaven is love.

SIR WALTER SCOTT

Time is too slow
for those who wait,
too swift for those who fear,
too long for those who grieve,
too short for those who rejoice;
but for those who love,
time is eternity.

HENRY VAN DYKE

'Tis said of love that it sometimes goes, sometimes flies; runs with one, walks gravely with another; turns a third into ice, and sets a fourth in a flame: it wounds one, another it kills: like lightning it begins and ends in the same moment: it makes that fort yield at night which it besieged but in the morning; for there is no force able to resist it.

MIGUEL DE CERVANTES

All thoughts,
all passions, all delights,
Whatever stirs this mortal frame,
All are but ministers of Love,
And feed his sacred flame.

SAMUEL TAYLOR COLERIDGE

The weight of
the world is love.
Under the burden of
solitude, under the burden
of dissatisfaction.

ALLEN GINSBERG

The commandment is that
you shall love, but when you
understand life and yourself,
then it is as if you should not need
to be commanded, because to love
human beings is still the only thing
worth living for; without this life
you really do not live.

Søren Kierkegaard

Love, and do what thou wilt: whether thou hold thy peace, through love hold thy peace; whether thou cry out, through love cry out; whether thou correct, through love correct; whether thou spare, through love do thou spare: let the root of love be within, of this root can nothing spring but what is good.

SAINT AUGUSTINE

When I hate,
so take I something from myself;
when I love,
so become I so much the
richer, by what I love.

FRIEDRICH VON SCHILLER

Forgiveness is the recovery
of an alienated property –
hatred of man a prolonged suicide;
egoism the highest poverty
of a created being.

FRIEDRICH VON SCHILLER

Love's over-brimming
mystery joins death and life.
It has filled my cup of pain
with joy.

RABINDRANATH TAGORE

Love does not
delight in evil but
rejoices with the truth.
It always protects,
always trusts,
always hopes,
always perseveres.
Love never fails.

1 Corinthians 13:6-8a (NIV)

Love takes off masks
that we fear we
cannot live without
and know we cannot
live within.

JAMES BALDWIN

One is loved
because one is loved.
No reason is needed
for loving.

PAULO COELHO

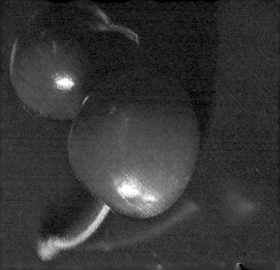